COLDPLAY
A RUSH OF BLOOD TO THE HEAD

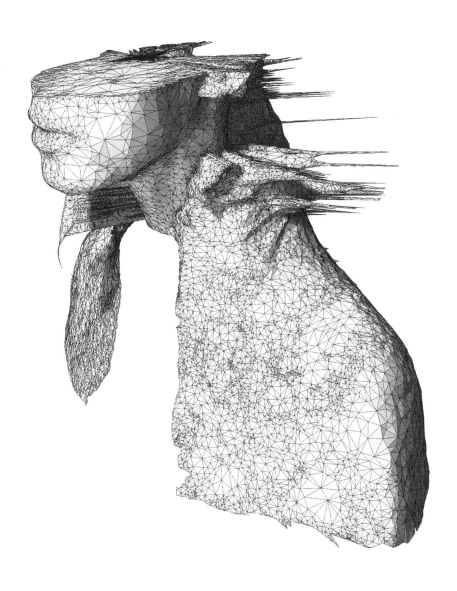

Wise Publications
London / New York / Paris / Sydney / Copenhagen / Berlin / Madrid / Tokyo

Exclusive distributors:

Music Sales Limited
8/9 Frith Street, London W1D 3JB,
England.

Music Sales Pty Limited
120 Rothschild Avenue, Rosebery, NSW 2018,
Australia.

Order No. AM975139
ISBN 0-7119-9606-7
This book © Copyright 2002 by Wise Publications.

Music arrangements by Derek Jones.
Music processed by Paul Ewers Music Design.
Cover artwork courtesy of Blue Source.

Printed in the United Kingdom by
Caligraving Limited, Thetford, Norfolk.

www.musicsales.com

Politik 5
In My Place 10
God Put A Smile Upon Your Face 14
The Scientist 21
Clocks 26
Daylight 32
Green Eyes 39
Warning Sign 45
A Whisper 52
A Rush Of Blood To The Head 57
Amsterdam 65

Politik

Words & Music by Guy Berryman, Jon Buckland, Will Champion & Chris Martin

Verse 2:
Give me one, 'cause one is best
In confusion confidence
Give me peace of mind and trust
Don't forget the rest of us.
Give me strength, reserve, control
Give me heart and give me soul
Wounds that heal, and cracks that fix
Tell me your own politik.

And open up your eyes *etc.*

In My Place

Words & Music by Guy Berryman, Jon Buckland, Will Champion & Chris Martin

1. In my place, in my____ place were lines that I____ could-n't
(Verse 2 see block lyric)

Verse 2:
I was scared, I was scared
Tired and under-prepared
But I'll wait for it.
And if you go, if you go
And leave me down here on my own
Then I'll wait for you, yeah.

Yeah, how long must you wait *etc.*

13

God Put A Smile Upon Your Face

Words & Music by Guy Berryman, Jon Buckland, Will Champion & Chris Martin

1. Where do we go, no-bo-dy knows.___
(Verses 2 & 3 see block lyrics)

I've got to say I'm on my way_____ down.

God give me style and give me grace.__

God put a

smile up-on my face._____

your guess_____ is as good___ as_____

mine._____

Guitar

Verse 2:
Where do we go to draw the line?
I've got to say I wasted all your time honey, honey
Where do I go to fall from grace?
God put a smile upon your face, yeah.

Verse 3:
Where do we go, nobody knows
Don't ever say you're on your way down, when
God gave you style and gave you grace
And put a smile upon your face.

Now when you work it out *etc.*

The Scientist

Words & Music by Guy Berryman, Jon Buckland, Will Champion & Chris Martin

1. Come up to meet__ you, tell you I'm sor - ry, you don't know how love-
(Verse 2 see block lyric)

No-bo-dy said__ it was ea-sy.__ Oh, it's__ such a shame

__ for us to part,_____ No-bo-dy said__ it was ea-sy.____

__ No-one ev-er said__ it would be this__ hard.__
(so)__

Oh, take me back to the start.____
(I'm go-ing)

Verse 2:
I was just guessing at numbers and figures
Pulling your puzzles apart.
Questions of science, science and progress
That must speak as loud as my heart.
Tell me you love me, come back and haunt me
Oh, and I rush to the start
Running in circles, chasing our tails
Coming back as we are.

Nobody said it was easy *etc.*

Clocks

Words & Music by Guy Berryman, Jon Buckland, Will Champion & Chris Martin

1. The lights go out and I can't be saved,
(Verse 2 see block lyric)
tides that I tried to

And no - thing else com - pares.

And no - thing else com - pares.

Verse 2:
Confusion that never stops
The closing walls and the ticking clocks
Gonna come back and take you home
I could not stop that you now know, singing…
Come out upon my seas
Cursed missed opportunities
Am I a part of the cure?
Or I am a part of the disease, singing…

You are etc.

Daylight

Words & Music by Guy Berryman, Jon Buckland, Will Champion & Chris Martin

And the clouds

burst   to show

day - - - - light.

Ooh,   and the sun   will shine.

Yeah,_____ on this heart___ of mine.

Ooh,_____ and I re - al - ise.

Who_____ can - not live___ with - out.

Ooh_____ come a - part___ with - out?

Verse 2:
On a hilltop
On a sky-rise
Like a first-born child
On the full tilt
And in full flight
Defeat darkness
Breaking daylight.

Ooh and the sun will shine *etc.*

Green Eyes

Words & Music by Guy Berryman, Jon Buckland, Will Champion & Chris Martin

came here with a load_____ and it feels so_____ much light-

-er_____ now I met_____ you._____

And ho-ney you___ should know that I could nev-er go_____ on_____

Verse 2:
Honey, you are the sea
Upon which I float
And I came here to talk
I think you should know
That Green Eyes
You're the one that I wanted to find
And anyone who tried to deny you
Must be out of their mind.

Because I came here with a load *etc.*

44

Warning Sign

Words & Music by Guy Berryman, Jon Buckland, Will Champion & Chris Martin

warn - ing___ sign,___ I___missed the good part then I

(Verse 2 see block lyric)

*1° Tacet till *

re - al - ised.___ I___ start - ed look - ing and the

bub - ble___ burst.___ I___ start - ed look - ing for ex -

- cu - ses.___

let_____ you_____ go.

Oh._____

So I

crawl_____ back_____ in - to_ your op - en__ arms._ Yes_ I

Verse 2:
A warning sign
You came back to haunt me
And I realised that you were an island
And I passed you by
When you were an island to discover.

Come on in
I've got to tell you what a state I'm in
I've got to tell you in my loudest tones
That I started looking for a warning sign.

When the truth is I miss you *etc.*

A Whisper

Words & Music by Guy Berryman, Jon Buckland, Will Champion & Chris Martin

A whis - per,___ a whis - per,___ a whis - per,___ a whis - per.___

I hear the sound___ of the tick - ing of clocks, who re - mem - bers your face___ who re -

mem - bers you when you are gone.

a whis - per,___ a whis - per,___ a whis - per,___ a whis - per.___

To Coda ⊕

Night_____ turns to day.___ And I still have these ques - tions.

Brid - - ges will break.___ Should I go

A Rush Of Blood To The Head

Words & Music by Guy Berryman, Jon Buckland, Will Champion & Chris Martin

- ble and fall ___ on my face. ___ And I know ___ the mis - takes ___ that I've ___ made. ___

___ See it all ___ dis - ap - pear ___ with - out a trace. ___ And they call ___

___ as they beck - on ___ you on. ___ They said start ___ as you mean ___ to go ___ on. ___

Oh, meet me on___ the road, oh, meet me where___ I___ said. Blame it all___ up-on___ a rush of blood___ to the head.

Amsterdam

Words & Music by Guy Berryman, Jon Buckland, Will Champion & Chris Martin

1. Come on,___ oh,

my star is fad - ing and I_____ swerve out of con - trol._____

If_____ I'd_____ if I'd on - ly wait - ed I'd not be stuck here in this__

_____ hole._____

2. Come here, oh,
(Verse 3 see block lyric)

and all a - round,   no it's no cause   for con - cern.

To Coda ⊕

D.S. al Coda

68

Stuck on the end_
of this ball and chain___
and I'm on my way___ back down

Verse 3:
Come on, oh, my star is fading
And I see no chance of release
And I know I'm dead on the surface
But I am screaming underneath.

And time is on your side *etc.*

3/03 (47085)